Things I Lost Along the Way

A Collection of Poems
by ~~John Wood~~

[signature]

God Bless You!
Thank You!

John Wood/SW Poetry LLC
www.spokenwoodpoetry.com
Cover Art by Sage Guillory
Book Design by Raheem Thompson

Publisher's Note: This is a work of fiction. Names, characters, places, and incidents are a product of the author's imagination. Locales and public names are sometimes used for atmospheric purposes. Any resemblance to actual people, living or dead, or to businesses, companies, events, institutions, or locales is completely coincidental.

Things I Lost Along the Way/ John Wood. -- 1st ed.
ISBN-13: 978-1542413831

Thank you, God,
For Your grace and Your love.
You renew my Spirit every single day.

For the family You blessed me with
From Headland to the hedges.
For friends who supported me, came to my shows,
and read my work up to this point
For anyone that had a part in crafting this book —
Raheem, Andre, Malik, Robert.

My parents, John and Iris
My sister, Irisa and my best friend, Steph
My mentor, Sam West

Every poet who has ever bled on a page.
Thank you, Jasmine Mans,

I love you all dearly.

Contents

Find It

"Every second of the search is an encounter with God"
Paulo Coelho

The Waves

To the water. How it accepts us in any condition

It is no secret that
I've spent most of my life hiding.
Blending.
Clinging desperately to the chords
that could whisk me away from these organs.
Forged my esteem in crowds, in-crowds.
Clenched a bogus smile until it put
a hole in both sides of my face.

                                        Lord knows.

My biggest regret is
never commissioning my hands to build
something to run with or run to.
But I did manage to master the assembly of arch,
the suspension of *here goes nothing*,
and the gristle file of nails
dulling this ark for the impact.

                        Listen, there is no music playing here.
                                But there is sound.

Mumblings of feet trying to lose themselves,
shrieking of girls who put their faith in accessories,
boats coaching their oars to hustle,
plummeting anchors disguised as bodies,

3

and the howling of canines and nines.

                                        This is no home of mine.

No wonder your answers couldn't save me.
Most men are not sanctuaries,
just monuments,
relics of a time that they cannot revisit,
frozen figures of movements that never began,
nomads who made deserts of their spoils,
And what a tragedy it must be to turn a mirage
into a destination.

                                            This is why.

I choose the water.
Indigenous soldiers who never ask
your fire about its origin,
your oars about their mileage.
They do not inquire about the bridges
you've casted into their bellies
Or why your clothes caress you
like they are holding secrets in their threads.

                        It is not their job to move us,
            but it is their pleasure to partake in movement.
                        And we do not know their notions,
                            but we trust their neutrality,
                    their contract with nature to harbor us.

4

This dive is the dialogue of the lost,
sinking of soul before the sinking of self,
the bubbling of fear's last laugh.
It is the metronome of the found,
the faithful and faithless,
the unity of purpose under the sun.

                                    Lord knows.

It is no secret that I am running,
hiding from something with or within me.
But like old relatives, the waves do not ask.
And sometimes, we do not need
to be questioned, only welcomed.
Embrace as wide as the shoreline.

                    When we resort to the cliff,
                    even if it is our last resort,
                    waging our suits as collateral,
                    we commission gravity
                    to relinquish us of our worry,
                    the rapids to wash us of our plunder.

But most importantly,
we give the sand permission
to transform our remains
into the incomparable treasures
that adorn the beach.

Silly of Me

My cologne reeks of insecurity.
        My acne scars mark that of pain.
Misunderstanding chaps my lips.

I heard myself speak for the first time
        in a long time the other day.
I stopped paying attention when the story
        brought me memories of men
that I pledged to never listen to again.

I cannot expect a woman to buy into a man
        who is still trying to separate his
whats from his *whys*...

I still haven't forgiven myself for the last time.

My tone has learned to harmonize with every
        See you later and *I'm sorry* that I was a
fool enough to believe.

I hope to find my way.
        As they appear to have found theirs.

My posture is oddly familiar and
        my smile has told endless lies.
The sort that many have majored in.
        But for some reason. Some ridiculous reason.
They still want to know my story.

Stomach Aches

To the stages I turned into altars and boys who are half man, half monster

I

And what of this stomach?
     A cauldron stewing its acid,
       wielding what the skin would consider foe.
I, too, coddle my beast,
     subdue it before I exit my lair
     in the mornings.

Some context here.
     It's junior year and
     a change of major is well overdue.
My friends are beginning
     to greet me like my associates.
One thing's for sure,
     I am not the boy I was two years ago.
His name brutally corroded.
I hear they still parade the gossip
     off their rosy gums.

Two things for certain.
I am still a vessel whether
     the gorge lies empty or full.
The spotlight discredits process.
We must begin bending our necks
     to digest the angle of remission,
     to count the crooked as straight in the eyes.

II

The sacrifice commences my bones,
    starting in the toes and then flaming the throat.
Woe is the watchman; he bows his head for grace
    and there is much to swallow here.
This mob leaves no deed unjudged and undead.
The truth is counted myth.
It is neither swollen or sharp enough for the ear's appetite.
    I deliver this lyrical plea only to watch it plummet
    on deaf souls.

What left but the foulness of gas?
Embarrassment wreaking in the smoke intensifies their
smug.
Air thick as countryside.
After the stomach has finished its bidding,
    we must concur with its jealousy of the womb.
It is more tool than tailor,
    no praise to be offered when its job is complete.

Long after the roar of the crowd,
    I try to pamper the abdomen's perpetual growl.
And while I do not remember the last time I ate,
        I let this be a reminder that
            there is still some beast in this flesh.
There is still more gnashing to be done,
    more burnings required to nurse the terror.

And what do we have left?
Choices, you say.
It is no dream of mine to sit with myself,
      better yet beside myself.
When I return home, Leviathan awakens.
He bids more stroke, more surrender of my growth.

III

So what of change?
The discomfort after the teeth nicks the tongue?
My God, the ache it creates.
      The position we assume,
          fetal and bowed.
It is the betrayal in honesty that sickens us,
      the inability to digest the guilt of the mouth.

There is no freedom where there is no confession.
Only torment's culpable pleasure,
      a lion that circles its dinner as if to seduce it.

When asked,
      Why do you hold your stomach when you perform?
        This orifice, an empty tomb of display,
          a voice not its own snags
            my esophagus and replies,
Don't you see the rivets on this body? It still needs me.

Interlude 1

A Break for Stomach Aches

What are stomach aches? A stomach ache is the discomfort that occurs while we are in the process of change, the anxiety that sickens us. It is the rumbling in the pit of your spirit that says *this is the hard part* and asks *what are you going to do?* It signals the accuser in the mind to tell us that we have not changed and persuades us to go back to the habits we are trying to leave behind.

What is the beast? The beast is any emotion or attitude we carry that may destroy future intimacy or promotion. And by intimacy, I mean the ability to share yourself wholeheartedly with others. It could be your temper, jealousy, complacency or the feeling of unworthiness. In most cases, the beast takes on the life of the accuser, especially if we listen to it. The accuser is also a persuader. He will say whatever it takes to keep us the same. We must always be cautious of the voices we are listening to because all war starts between the ears. For me it was guilt, lust, un-forgiveness, and shame. Every time I stepped on a stage, there was a part of me that I could not share, and I didn't understand why. It manifested physically in my stance -- one arm lay clinched around my stomach as if to protect it. The stomach and the beast were doing a number on both my mind and my heart.

10

What are the rivets? The rivets are any bridges or hinges we create to keep us close to the beast. These could be physical places, insecurities, excuses, or thought patterns. If there is a person who turns us into the beast, then the rivets could be a sexual relationship or something as simple as a text thread. As long as the rivets remain, the beast keeps its access to us and our wounds. It doesn't matter how much space we may have created or how *over it* we claim to be.

It is hard to control the beast and even harder to destroy the rivets. In a sense, they become a part of us. We own them and call the pollution our personality. My personal life frequently bled onto the stage. It was the only truth I had access to, but it was one of many truths that I could not fully grasp. The wisdom I spoke did not carry much weight because my life did not reflect the portrait I was painting. People knew who I was -- especially my mistakes. The stage subsequently became my altar. It became a place I could go to sacrifice my guilt and shame to myself, my listeners, and my Creator. After shows, I would go home, reflect, and make plans to work on myself. But it wasn't enough. I was not ready to let go.

The goal:
Control the stomach. Conquer the beast. Destroy the rivets.

Sick Days

Living like this on six days
  is turning my Sundays into sick days.

Ignoring sermons from the Reverend.
  Nowadays I don't even feel worthy enough to
  be in Your presence.

Perhaps I am too dirty to be cleaned,
  Taste of liquor on my breath when I sing.

Unsure of which master I've been serving,

And perhaps it's so hard for me to accept Your love
  Because I've been too busy trying to deserve it.

Deserving

To the boys my father was a father to

No one ever told him that he didn't
have to hold his chest so high.
And that while a man may advertise his horsepower,
there's no shame in admitting that
there is still work to be done under the hood.

When superman and men in jerseys are
the only role models you have to look up to,
how can we expect our boys to understand
that they do not need superpowers to deserve love
and that consistency is far more precious than
performance?

No one ever showed him
how to hold his head.
Because only men with dope stained hands
could massage their egos.
Not enough occasions for tucked shirts
or creased pants.
No one to show him how to hold the ball in his hands.

No one ever taught him how to ride a bike,
so, he never dreamed of running away from home.
Instead, he learned to laugh through disappointment
and tuck his tears into his fears.
He taunts what he does not understand,
holds his words captive to his insecurities.

No one ever taught him to revere a woman's smile
or the proper time to hold her hand
and that silence is way more powerful than
a battered tongue.
Instead, he aspired to collect their hearts
like his cousins collected their guns,
heavy as caskets with the desire to be held.

No one ever taught him how to talk to God
when you didn't feel like He was listening.
And if they did, he wasn't listening.
A child gets tired of unanswered questions,
of waiting by the fireplace
to see if daddy is really Santa,
to prove to the other kids
That the only reason they didn't think he was real
was because they didn't have daddies either.

No one ever told them that we needed them.
That someone from our hood was supposed to
see us dance across the stage,
that they were supposed go
back home and rescue boys like them,
and that they were blooded in Christ way
before they ever claimed their sets.

I wish they believed me when I said I understood.
But while car rides may be deceiving,
roads are not.
Our worlds would never be quite as tight as
our daps or as affectionate as our hugs.

I'll Admit It

I'll admit it.
I'm guilty of being an actor
in stories that I never planned to finish.

Tryouts

Lately, I find myself
    counting down the days for you to be mine.
And I would usually comfort myself by saying that
    time is on our side
        But I am no fool,
        falling for fairytale fallacies.
It simply is not.

We are, but, aspiring actors searching for our big break
    Putting it all at stake.
        Dreaming,
            hoping to push our souls through
            these lines before our time is up,
            auditioning for a show that we know
            so many other people are lined up for.
But we wait.

With tired feet, we
tie up our shoelaces
hoping it will prevent us from tripping,
        while your curious eyes judge
          That the mud from our last destination
    won't stain the newly renovated floors.
With strained hearts and minds
    we muster up enough courage to show you,
    and, only you, that this is natural.

Like we didn't blow off friends
   and ruin fun plans just to practice what we would say if
   we ever got this moment.
       Only for them to ask,
           Why is this so important to you?
       And we confidently reply,
           This one is special.

A dream unfulfilled has a way of
   giving your subconscious a to-do list while it rests
And it will never diminish
   until it tastes the rubber marks of success.
We have lost sleep over this gig.

So, with reddened eyes,
   we look for your acceptance,
   your essence, that we are indeed the perfect fit for this
   role.
       I suppose that I'll be whoever you want me to
       be.
It will only make it easier for me to lose myself in
   character.
       I'll even laugh at your corny jokes
       just to become a credit in your Heath ledger.
       It would be my pleasure.

Because your script is like the Word on a Sunday morning.
                   And these scenes have become
                   the honey, milk, and cream
                   of my daydreams.
So I act,
   anything to get a call back.
I perform,

anything for a chance to be in your arms.
I audition,
   anything to put us in a better position
And in silence, I wait.

Fidgeting from my spirit to my bones,
                I wait.
Like sitting through long prayers on Thanksgiving Day,
                I wait.
For your response,
   your reaction,
   your complete satisfaction.

Leaving it on the stage,
staring at the competition as I shut the doors casually.

Waiting for the call
   so, I can tell you that

I would be honored to play the hero in this tragedy.

An Ode to New Earth

For BUGA
After Joshua Bennett

Our mouths watered of sativa, poisonous nectar,
and the last 5 dollars we had for 4 days.
Behold a New Earth, tithe me a dance or
a pole I can shift my burdens to.
Where fences ain't boundaries and
crushes ain't fear factors.
Yeaaa, oh let's do it!

I find myself practicing the lines in my grin,
mischievous, ill intentions
cascading across the church parking lot.
How did we get here?
My last recollection, blurry shades of
redness and the sneakers of the boy who
made the hunch punch.

A belch rattles my poise,
as I notice we are down one soldier.
Our fantasies are at war here.
Let us not come undone.
Pledged our allegiance to thighs,
viral dances, and Waka.

An ode to the hero,
combating the bane of our existence
transformed untapped airwaves into
fire tones, Dougherty Street into Arkham.

Make way for the girls who
captivate the cadence with their hair flips,
    divas trembling floorboards with the sway of their
      hips.
Make room for the men whose
whistles usher rhythm into existence,
the klan who baptized their shoulders in blade
Watch out for the pack who traded their hands
for hooks.

Play a song for the boys who minored in
twisted wrists and the shuffle of handclaps
Speakers shatter the countenance of chords,
a sea of quivering legs and uncaged hips
counteract whiskey bent denials and
minority reports.

My friends hold my torso as if I'm in a fight
while I try to get a handle on this mountain
of magnificence.

Bruh, this is a ceremony.
A lifting of yesterday's struggles,
A sacrifice of tonight's memories.
Hustle them atop the stage.
Give their coins a language of gratefulness.

Take that damsel home,
She is much too toxic for this celebration.
I've committed to this synchronization of hips
until the end of this song.
These bare hands temper their urges

as I prepare my speech for the let out.
The sidewalk is known to separate the boys
from the men.

This here is not a drill.
It is the molding of makeshift romance.
The bonding that Saturday morning
recaps are made of.
Add some pimp to your lips.

Much love to the place,
that gave our feet a home to dance,
our embarrassment a grave.
Round of applause,
Baby,
to the place that gave college its
Cs and its LOLs.

Truth Is

To the women who have danced hopelessly in the margins of my notebook

Have I ever
  told you that it was my fault?
That I have denied love every time
  it opened its arms to me.

Have I ever
  told you why they hate me?
That I could sport a lie like the
  truth was on crutches.

Have I ever
  told you where they went?
That they hide outside the margins of my notebook.
  And on some nights,
They muster up enough courage to show up
  on a line.

Have I ever
  told you how I said goodbye?
That I have yet to say it,
  And closure is a chapter in
our book that we never reached.

Have I ever
  told you why they cried to me?
That a broken heart has no bedtime,
  it shakes you out of your sleep
Rejects your dreams again.

Have I ever
   told you that they haunt me in my dreams?
And that guilt is a drug,
   I've overdosed on a million nights.

Have I ever told you
that I always knew
you would end up
just like
them?

2am

About four times a year...
My guilt's lust for freedom imbibes my brain's BAC.
My heart's broken dreams, scattered in different parts of
my soul, resurface,
Stretching the pieces that rest in my hands as if they had
only been asleep.
My fingertips memory jog the depths of my phone.
They search for unfinished conversations and unanswered
questions.
My ears listen with patience, stirring my blood in
confusion, rushing to my chest
Waves of preparedness.
I pause in the surprise of a reluctant,
Hello
I speak in Gin,
I enunciate in Rum,
I swallow saliva of disappointment
Only to throw up my good intentions.
I Google *recipes for regret hangovers*
No results found.

Tin Man

To the men who are still trying to catch a breath of forgiveness

Fight for another chance to be with you?
I promise I would.
If I could hold the entire universe in my hand,
it would never be enough if you weren't in my space.
Just to taste, the sweet sensors of your skin again
is a dream that will never come true.
Knew that I was a fool for refusing to play by the rules.
But, I was never a teacher's pet.

Instead, I'll just let the memories of my past
puncture holes in the middle of my soul.
To watch the shadows of my feet
make peace with their maker,
staggering into a reality that I can't accept.

IT'S A WRECK, to sail into the seas of love
to shipwreck on the islands of loneliness.
I was never equipped to take the trip.
I could never be the captain of the boat
or a member of the crew
swimming thousands of miles just to be with you.

I was drowning in a pit of lies
when I inserted myself into your thighs.
I stole the keys to your heart and
put them into someone else's ignition.
PUSH TO START my ignorance.

When you dig up my remains,
I won't even have a brain.
And the tombstone will read:

He died dancing in his pride. Moving to the beat of his ego,
he collapsed trying to hold in everything that was inside.
With him is buried all the hearts of the women
that he hurt and cursed. Piling him with dirt,
he would never breathe the fresh breath of forgiveness.

I'm sorry for a being fool.

Signed,

The Man With No Heart

Butterflies No More

Baby, you give me butterflies, inside...
Not really but I wish you did.
When I was a kid, I used to ponder at the rules of the
playground where we played house.
And your spouse was always that girl you really liked
In spite of the fact that you might have crushed on others
in the class and now as times pass...
I wonder if I'll ever see the maturity of things that I
thought were so sure to be.
Looking back, I was naive to believe that this was as easy
to retrieve
As the stories I read in books and saw on TV.
I had to realize that there is no indentation for different
relations
When the sole purpose of our conversation
was for penetration.
How are we going to build trust out of lust?
Playing games, guessing all the wrong letters just to hang
our hearts from a noose.
When the truth is that it's not so easy trying to check your
pride
When your muscles are filled with ALL THIS JUICE that
don't even give you nourishment.
Searching for the fruit of your long lost Eve, we will dive

And dive into your gardens even when we know we're not
ready for the seed.
But if you really listened, you would notice that his game
was faintly hissing.
Shedding his old skin with new lies
I used to want to save my virginity
Until I felt the fireworks on the inside.
How dumb was I?
And I used to be so sure that you were the one
Until I put my hands in the waters and realized this had
only just begun and now,
I don't even get butterflies no more.
I don't even know where to begin.
When she used to touch on me, I used to long to feel the
senses of happiness and satisfaction through her skin, it
was never only about getting it in, but feeling like I was
her superman gave me true satisfactions within.
Do you remember when we used to touch the
constellations on summer flights?
Or when we would explore excerpts of your fantasies all
through the night...
Just to wrap myself around the blanket of your mind gave
me the time to appreciate the real you, and the smallest
whist of your scent made all my time feel well spent...
But you're telling me that I can get the skins as Clark Kent?
Seeking the personal perks of a jerk, he acclimated to the
system of putting in work based on your worth.
First! You a fool to play by the rules.

Second! There are no rules. Only sex, games, and lies, and any way to get into them thighs is what the homies said, *Scoring ain't for lovers but for the men who can make illusions of love in the bed.*

Well said, you have now been filled with the seeds of deceit and it's time to reap the questions of all the thots that's been planting themselves within your reach.

You got that stupid look on your face but
is this not what you wanted?

But seriously I don't even get butterflies no more.

Them old R&B tracks don't mean nothing to me no more.

Not MJ, not Boyz II Men, not Brian, and it's always too much for Luther.

I'm still waiting on someone to tell me the point of making the dive of love if you don't feel the butterflies in your stomach when you drop

It's not even a roller coaster anymore.

Why would I give my all to the fall when I have nothing to make sure I stay there?

I must've lost a piece of my soul diving into those walls, making house calls to quench the warm creases of the desert, measured my manhood in a lie that this would bring me complete satisfaction. They should change the laws of attraction to the laws of personal satisfaction.

I often wonder, who taught young men
how to objectify women?

And ladies, he ain't gone run no laps for you when he's only interested in swimming.

I wanted to open her seas with my hands

but I ain't Moses.
I lost track of who I was, I started to lose focus.
A tornado flew around in my room
as they went and came.
And it amazes me how men will do women the dirtiest just
to gain some homeboy fame.
Searching for them butterflies
after he demonized his skies.
But my dawg was a victim, he was simply ill advised.
Your past has the funniest ways of haunting you.
Insecurities you buried will resurrect and start
taunting you.
I remember when I was drowning.
I was downing myself in so much filth
Now I can't even get down with you
because I'm drowning in guilt.
Don't choose to climb into them whack trees
You ain't ever gone leave them rotten leaves.
And how easily it is to become Icarus during
metamorphosis.
But I was a lucky one...
The Lord tapped me on my shoulder,
See you older, you got a choice to be a soldier,
And it's your choice to follow my will cuz son,
I can't control you. You have to choose to be true.
Falling to them tricks, he ended up
losing face, love and time,
Realized while he was lending fornication,
He was only degrading his mind.

P.S. Don't give yourself to everybody.

Battle Cry

It is written that
He endured great anguish before the cross.
Is this why the battle cries even when the
war has only just begun?

Being Mortal

To the loved ones we wish God would've let stay with us a little longer
And the doctors who nursed them to glory

I thought that I would become better at this. But time has shown me that I'm just as weak as the people I must stand strong for. And no matter how many times I wash my hands, I can never seem to rinse off the anxiety that comes with bad news. I have run out of lies to tell myself. Fear has never looked so pristine. How can a place that looks so clean personify so many nightmares? To be honest, after seeing so many people cry tears, you can get used to anything. And if Hell is this close, I can only imagine that Heaven is but a mile away. I have watched them as they face their fears. Calendar dates that they will never see. IVs and dosages that will never set them free. And medicine rooms are like the laughing stocks of cancer, echoing prayers of victims that were never answered.

I have seen the way they look at me. A superhero who has just lost his powers. The ticking hours are his kryptonite. I have seen the stages. Denial, hope, acceptance, because saving graces never seemed to visit them or remain constant in their presence. I can imagine that closed doors resemble corridors that they must soon face. Chasing away thoughts that I have never been able to escape. I try my best to forget when I go home. I try my best to help them fight to the end. But every day I come to terms with the fact that the fight against mortality is not one that we were ever meant to win.

To Breathe

To the love I've hoarded for myself,
I have identified most of it as pride.

To the pride I've replaced people with,
Its aroma is suffocating me.

To the breaths I've taken without you,
I am still waiting to take one.

Just Breathe

These are the moments that will make or break you. The discomfort we feel when the tough moments arise do not come to hurt us but rather remind us. They remind us that the new us hasn't yet settled in. There is still more understanding required, more conversations to be held, more growth to be done. It is a reminder that God is still at work and that the truth He has left standing at the door of our hearts still does not have permission to come in. And it will not barge in. It must be welcomed. Our minds are still in the process of renewing.

No one needs to tell us that we need to change or that we need to kill an unhealthy habit. You may be one of the people who already knows why your friends keep dropping you, why you can't keep a good girl around, why your finances are in a rut, why you keep getting fired, or why people are scared to tell you the truth. You may already know and you just need to fix it. That's a much better position be in. That should be some motivation to put it to work. But if you are like some, you don't know why.

If you do not know, let me help. Let's self-reflect a little. What is the reoccurring habit? Take some time to think about it. Is it lashing out, overspending, infidelity, carrying baggage, anger, self-doubt, or jealousy? This is the hard part, so it will take some thinking. What typically happens right before the behavior occurs? Is everyone saying the same thing? Surely everyone you know couldn't be wrong (and of course we would like to think that they are). Occasionally, the hardest part about fixing a problem is finding the problem. Any doctor, nurse, mechanic or IT professional can endorse that message. Plus, we get pretty good at hiding it under our excuses or whatever version of the truth we tell people who can't see the first-hand encounter. The key to getting to the bottom of this is identifying the pattern. The pattern will lead you to the problem. Really take some time to look inward. This could take days or weeks to figure out.

Research. Grab a good friend, preferably one who does not have the same issue or who has conquered it. People who have conquered fear are typically good at pointing it out. People who have great relationships with God are usually good at pointing out pitfalls of those who don't. The same goes for marriage and relationships. No friends? (not being funny here) That's fine too. Find a good book, scripture, or forum on the behavior or pattern you are noticing. Sometimes this will be your only ally. If you have never had a friend suffer from depression, then it could be hard to talk to them about the issue. Hash it all out and ask yourself the questions. Let your guard down so that you can accept any truths that arise from these interactions.

Why does this bring me so much discomfort? Why can't I get away from this thing or these types of people? Like the scripture says, "Seek and you will find" (*Matthew 7:7*). This step is one of the most important. God's presence is guaranteed, but His will for your life is not. There are some things that need to go and we can't let them go if we don't know what they are. When the stomach aches come, just breathe. Breathe in and breathe out; remember that this is all a part of the process.

Leave It

"Every road, after a few miles, forks into two...
into two again, and at each fork you must make a decision.
Life is not like a river but like a tree....
Creatures grow further apart as they increase in
perfection"
C.S. Lewis

SWATS

I
Lingo larger than locked jaws
Roads that bump like 12s in rear ends
Tips black and mild or unsolicited
Loud that falls on deaf ears
Pants that no longer know waists
Chains that memorize heartbeats
Thugs
Boys
Men
Niggas
Girls who want street niggas
Women who are almost tired of them
Junkies who don't need teeth to tell their stories
Stoplights that have slept with stick-up kids
Kids too ready to stick up for their hoods
Sirens that come a little too late
Babies that arrive a little too early
Salons that add sass to seduction
Foreigners who don't care to know the history
of this neighborhood

II
Boys who encouraged us to be Outkasts
Men who would rather die than to be reborn on the
Eastside
Thugs who thug for the sake of thugging
Risks we used to skate at them
Wings serious business
Noise that is organized
Music my cheeks can brag about
Gentleman's clubs, ain't no gentlemen in this poem
Trap house, mom's house or abandoned building
Streets that run parallel to struggles
Niggas born wolf or tiger
Feed the pack
Earn stripes feeding yourself
2 cousins from the 3
5 cousins from the 4
1 cousin from the 1
We only needed 1
Prophet Shawty-Lo for recognizing the two sides
Thugs
Boys
Men
Niggas

Boys who stopped
thugging to become men
so their sons wouldn't have
to be niggas again.

Old Mercedes

For John T.

My father's last was heavier, more brass
than any currency on this side of 20.
It was drenched in sweat, a struggle in it.
I don't know who I inherited these clammy
hands from, but father never got nervous
when the diligence in his palms met empty pockets.

Our car rides, bilingual coasts
My parents could never rid themselves of
the burden of tying yourself to your dreams.
My other half or greatest adversary,
depending on the chapter, treated back seats
like cell blocks, kill for your own space.

Magician is the parent who has every kid on
the block believing that Benjamins grow from your roots.
But I saw my parents pull a rabbit out of a
hat twice when a bill collector turned an
extension into an audacity and a dial tone into a forest fire.
I didn't know much about family trees but I could've
crossed my heart that God was our first cousin.

Most Saturdays I had a sweet tooth,
the crunch in a Snickers, the smoothness of a cruise,
the stickiness in an eavesdrop.
My heart observed

the humility that took vacation in his pride,
the decorum that upholstered his patience,
the disappointment that ran-a-muck in his anger.

My favorite,
the reluctance that persisted in his pitch when
he leaned over and said,
Baby, you got some more money?

Holy Ground

I grew up by the Church's in the churches but pews could never keep
us away from generational curses

At Christian school,
earned first stripes
by opening rebellious eyes during prayer

Like speeding on 285
see *them* before they see you
Write-ups, phone calls,
Displays like slave disciplining
In front of intimidated eyes
nervous about escaping

Usual suspects,
their parent's phones
dial tones or endless rings
Something about submission
about intimacy in raised hands
about sovereignty in praise

Or the absence thereof
Ain't ever seen no man they admired
praise God before
Ain't ever seen no boy profit
from surrender
Held their masculinity even on Holy ground

Still
faithless
fatherless in their prayers

Still raising their hands
bullets if you don't

Still on the ground
it just ain't holy no more

To the Teacher Who Left After the First Month of School

Always be kind. You never know what someone is going through.

A slew of children laughing at you
        buckled your knees.
I watched your breath look for oxygen
        that wasn't bending in the corral.
Chalk smoke rising at its pleasure.
        A desk mistook its legs for wings.
A door knock pounced like your heart
        was calling for assistance.

It is a shame that black children are so used
        to breaking our men or seeing them be broken
that we would gladly partake in the flogging.
        A child will not raise his hands for questions,
but buckle his fists for answers.

The audacity of my peers to disregard
        the black royalty on the walls,
to lynch our lesson.
        But we could not help our thirst
        for the quiver of weakness.
This is simply the coming of age,
        the craving to test the fierceness of one's roar.

The room lingered the next day when
        your desk echoed a hollow, empty note.
My classmate dropped her bottom lip like

46

your ego when the news rang across my
principal's lips like last period.

Years later, we would reminisce of your suffering.
        Embrace our regret like backpacks,
over the shoulders and under the arms.
        The cruelty in ignorance is enchanting.
We often expose our beast long before
        we meet our beauty.

I still search for arms strong enough
        to lift the bags under your eyes,
        mints sharp enough to cut the odor of shame.
Addiction can hide behind your shirt like Hanes.
        But broken men tend to shake a lot when
        there's no grace in the air.

Reminder: In Light of Trump

From Caves

Black children,
you are much more than
the caves this world will make of you,
much more than just caves to a nation
who may be too afraid or dismayed
by your skin tone to explore you.

Black boys, when they treat you like a cave,
intimidated by your shadow,
know that you are a bat cave.
Police, politicians, judges, courts,
will try to put caution tape on your lips,
don't be afraid to Bruce Wayne these Jokers.
Vigilantes ain't always meant to be understood.
Your Dark Knights are just miracles on the horizon.

Black girls, when they treat you like a cave
unpredictable yet so tempting,
know that you are a history undocumented,
crystal ceilings and magic in your hair unrevealed.
You are hand paintings of black queens,
Coretta Scott Kings,
the beauty outside the eyelids of *I Have a Dream*.

Black kids, girls, boys,
when you leave your porch,
I cannot promise that those
put in place to protect you, to justify you,
will not treat you like dangerous caves.

That they will not make horror stories
out of your mystery,
exploit it and call you entertainment.
Many will not be brave enough to
hold a flashlight to your truths so they can walk with you.

I cannot promise that you will be treated like
all the other things that this world has claimed to
but I encourage you to not let this world claim you.
While they only see an empty cave,
a barren space,
you must trust the writings
on the walls of your creativity
to speak the waterfalls of knowledge on your tongue.

Black children you are a monument of magnificence,
whether they take the time to explore you or not.

Boards and Boys

For Justin

Let's be like those boards,
Those boys,
Distinct as handprints.
The way we wear our pain.

Sweaty to our socks,
We still stretch with no shame.
Even though
Our chalk, our utensils,
Have been broken down, shared
Dissipated in the air...

Like those boards, like those boys
Let's erase,
Retry,
Erase and retry
And when erasers fail us,
We can use our hands.
If only to try again.

Like those boys,
Can we decide in an instant
that being alone is not as fun?
Because sometimes,
we need a home away from home.
A friend to take our hand, to hear our plans,
to signal us from the back of the classroom
to change our answers again.

Like those boards,
Will water and rags suffice?
Can we get ready for a new day?
Dim the lights.
Forget our attempts.
Make peace with those handprints.

Like those boards, like those boys
Can we decide that a new slate and a new day
will only make recess that much more sweet?

Black Barbie

To any girl who has ever called her doll her best friend

I can still feel all those eyes staring down at me.
Judging, at how boys were licensed to
to be careless with their valuables.
A boy could turn any still object into a toy if
he had enough time to test its resilience.
My grandmother hoarded Barbie dolls
like there was some piece of her childhood
that she could not outlive, that she wanted to admire daily,
amassing for every black girl who needed a foot-long
shrine in a nation of life-sized insecurities.
For every black child
who never learned to draw elegance with a brown crayon.
Her memory, crinkled victim of paper bag tests,
still gasping at how colorism restricted
the breadth of our identity.
I can still feel all those eyes staring down at me.
A spectacle for a social experiment I was unaware of.
Kin or Ken. Rusty hands on innocent fingertips
And melted chocolate was damaged goods
So I never revered the sweetness in a maybe
Only to scrub my hands of tragedies that could've been
Especially when they leave messes.
Figurines, toy trucks, and old cartridges never prepared

me to handle the fragility of girl who would spend
most of her life being robbed of her beauty marks.
Only taught me to push buttons.
Not an affinity for admiration or conduct in museum.
And black girls be like museums.
Last week, I watched my cousin carry a Barbie doll
with her to the bathroom.
Capitalizing on signature best friend qualities,
bathroom breaks, hair and nails sessions,
and occasional man investigations.

When all the women I ever loved
looked at me for the last time,
I could still feel all of them staring down at me.
In their cases, watching a boy be a boy again.
A boy who had yet to understand that some things
just can't be replaced.

To A Woman I Never Knew Pt. II

I haven't kissed anyone like this in a long time.
I am searching for parts of you that
my last lover didn't have.
Willing to taste your bitter and sweet buds.
Grip you while I can.
My soul jumps when you're around.
They leave messages in my eyes.
Is it okay that I am broken?
Still carrying a box with my pieces in them.
Can you hear them shake when I walk?
They are loud yet only few remain.
Will you hold them for me?
Pretend that I am whole.
I know that it's not your job to put them together
But can you hold them for me?
I promise that it won't be long.

My Perfect Simile

I love you like warm heat on winter nights
Like when cold air hits your insides
when the summer sun gets too bright.
Like a fresh piece of gum when the flavor is intense
The way locomotive motion of my jawline can taste buds
of your sweet nectar and send chills down my spine.
That's how much you get on my nerves.

Your eyes light up like July 4th.
And they watch me like the sparrow
And if there were more female Pharaohs,
I would petition the ancients to write
commentaries to their dignitaries
about your physical sanctuary.
Your waters flow like the Nile.
And your hair blows like the desert sand
and if you were a part of my caravan,

I wouldn't dare trade you for waters
that would quench my thirst
but lead me away from my promised land.
Your heartbeat sounds like orchestra symphonies.
And it don't matter if we listening to
Zaytoven or Beethoven,
your classy and sassy flow rip tracks
like piracy and they can remain stolen.
Like fresh CDs with the case opened,
you would be the producer of every hit in my booklet.
Or like when my favorite song from three years ago

comes on shuffle and reminds me that often times
Love is about the perfect moment, the perfect artist and
the perfect rhyme...

I love you like a handful of skittles with all the best colors,
like the warm side of the bed with all the covers.
I write to you like you're Nina and I'm Darius LoveHall.
And I will track you down just so I can bring rhythm to
your blues.
Awaken your heart and never put it on snooze.
And even though we've taken shots like Monica and
Quincy and we play hard,
you remind me that my heart is nothing but net and
there's no need to play guard.
Your smile pulls me like gravity
and even when you claim you're mad at me, it never
seems to knock us off our axis.

You fit me like closed hands with tight grips
that with friction would send prayers to a God who
embodies love and made us in His shadow and even
though we aren't on that plateau He sacrificed a part of
Himself so that it could be felt.
So, I wonder agape, what are you?
Are you a road trip with stops and maps but
no destination?
What are you made of?
Are you the perfect recipe with pictures and
ingredients but no mentions of necessities?
What will you say?
Do you speak Corinthian tongues or
do you trip over your speech from arguments with bae?

Scratch my back with road maps that will show me how to
get back to you if I lose my tracks.
Grip my mind with fingers that linger or grab my attention
like middle school Nokias when I heard my ringer.

You go good with everything like butter.
No wonder you got that perfect cake.
You surprise me like a low bill on a dinner date,
You save me from myself without a cape,
You run circles through my mind like a figure eight,
You look bad in Blaque,
You make it boom like an 808.
You got soul.

You are a perfect metaphor, a forever yours,
an I love to see you in a beautiful outfit
with a fresh pedicure...
whatever you got it's in me
And I guess you just like like like like like my perfect
simile.

Growing Apart

Was it Heaven at all?

I had a dream about Heaven the other night.
    Everything about it was perfect.
        But. You were nowhere to be found.

So, I left.
Because to me,
    you were the only thing that could complete it.

And I searched for you...
    with the intensity that any man who had just given up
    paradise would.

And when I was only inches away from touching your
    fingertips, hell-bent on bringing you back with me
    the dream abruptly ended.

Things I Should've Left

After Rudy Francisco

My sincerest apologies
To the people I tried to take with me,
To the women who thought I was the one,
To the love that I deemed a distraction.

My stomach has made peace with God's silence.
My palms sweat a little less when I pray.

Now I know that though your hands may be empty,
there are just some things that you can't take with you.

Acceptance

This is all that I have to give. This is all that I am. As a matter of fact, this is all that is left of me so in nakedness is where I stand. Is this enough for you? Actually, don't answer that....

I find myself puzzled at how grown-ups always tried to add structure to my childhood dreams that only wanted to flourish and beam, to break out of cocoons in their own season. Constructs always seem to construct parameters around things that were never meant to be controlled.

But I cannot blame them for their persistence, their love, we are only remnants of the love that we are given. I am still accepting the fact that the paintings they crafted with me as the subject matter were never meant to hang in museums. The reality that has forced me to wash my thoughts like Katrina's. Catastrophic baptisms. And now I hold belief that we can all be Mona Lisas.

Because life is the only canvas where we may choose to draw our art. It has a peculiar smile that every individual must interpret. Yet we can all agree that it is indeed a smile.

As the holidays approach, I lie anxious in the thought of not having you around. I guess it's because I've never done well with accepting gifts or was never convinced that external things are where my happiness should be found.

Acceptance is like looking toward December in January. There is some untold story between that time, but it's coming nevertheless. It is the aroma of freedom after nights of congestion, the hug of warmth after days of depression. It is the essence of self-love. The gift of yourself to yourself, the gentle wrapping of peace that can't be found in presents. But let us take notes.

At its worst, it is the crutch that allows fear to thrive in our lives. It is a false crown. A poison that infects our subconscious that cannot easily be found. Lethal injections of imperfection will not lend themselves to easy detection. Let's keep ourselves from the surgery that we must undergo when we place the wrong things inside of us and the body goes through rejection. Protection is key. Do not accept the wrong thoughts, the wrong energy, the wrong love, guarding our hearts is one of the most important jobs of the human soul. Let's accept God's love above all.

Affirming our gifts and talents is the greatest award, the most important call that we will ever pick up.

I reroute.

Is this enough for you?

To be completely honest, the answer to that question doesn't matter anymore.

Is this enough for me?

I'm learning to answer this every day, but I know that it is a question that I cannot ignore.

Is this enough for Him?

Well, I think that accepting His love for me, is the only thing He was waiting for.

Intersections

One of the best things that we are is
Not perfect.

But, we are imperfections in intersections
Looking for perfection in our purpose.

Eczema

To save me from myself,
I was made to wear gloves on my hands as a child.
Every time my godmother scolded me
for playing with my scabs,
resentment seared in my chest
like wine on an iron skillet.
Itching all too much like the plagues God reigned on
Egyptian families, my room sang like I
was trying to start a fire with stones.
My first line of defense left discolored, stubborn,
all too ready to bring attention to my leprosy.

My parents' faces, wrinkled like prunes
and I, like an alcoholic at an intervention,
was put on trial
for a disease, I didn't ask for.
I learned at the age of 8 that pain
could hurt so good and that
sometimes your limbs are not your friends.

My godmother's frustration was more obnoxious
than the volume of Saturday morning cartoons.
But, she was teaching me something
about scabs, about scars, about wounds
Picking at them only lengthened their stay.
Only gave them more ground
to lodge themselves in a grave I called my skin.
And maybe sometimes God can't do
what He wants with us
because we are too busy reopening our scabs.

It might get infected sounded too much like
Boy you might lose a limb.
But what do you do when a child's pain
becomes his comfort zone?
All too overt that we tampered with our scabs
too much, too long,
lost too many limbs, too much blood,
trying to hold on to too much pain.

I cannot speak for you,
but I am still learning how to
refrain from picking at my scabs.
I am still learning to allow my pain to
make peace with the rest of my skin.
To regrow the pieces of myself that
I lost with my infected limbs.

Asthma

Breathing with swollen airways is
much like waiting to relax during a horror film.
Diaphragm palpitating with the tics.

My prognosis, we are all inflicted with asthma.
Lungs pink pressured.
Gaps cluttered with dirt.
We make people our inhalers
Assuming they know how to treat our shortness of breath.

The Doctor is funny ain't He?
The way He stops filling our prescription
And forces us to learn how to breathe on our own.

delivered.

To blocked texts and the places your mind goes in light them

If you talk to her before I do,

Tell her
    that love is nothing more than
    a memory that is always relevant.
Tell her
    that she was the sweetener to my coffee
    on mornings that made me question why God woke me
    up.
Tell her
    that if love was a dead end,
    I would still take the trip as long as
    she was in my passenger seat.
And if I ever met God on a Sunday morning,
    I would commend Him on His creations and His
    patience in making someone who could give me that
    much motivation.
Tell her
    that goodbyes are like long love letters
    crushed into two syllables but it's critical
    that we follow His will even when it's the most difficult.

Delivered from the Rivet

rivet (n) - a short metal pin or bolt for holding together two plates of metal

lair (n) - a wild animal's resting place, especially one that is well hidden.

It's heavy isn't it? The un-forgiveness, the embarrassment, the shame, the anger you're carrying around. Or maybe it's the person you keep telling your friends you're going to drop, the friend who keeps betraying your trust, the homeboy who encourages you to be unfaithful or the family member that keeps using you. We all have our burdens, our monsters and don't these things always play well into our weaknesses? They play into our caring nature, our desire to be loved, our need to be validated, our insecurities, and sometimes it's just our pride. Some of us are used to carrying other people's problems. Some of us feel like we've already spent too much time with this person or doing this thing, and often we just feel stuck.

My story? I had an unhealthy relationship with myself and my craft. Not only was I changing in front of others at an alarming rate, but I was also committing self-sabotage. Poetry was my first love and it was the place I healed the most when I was unhappy with who and where I was. But, I became so used to being broken that I would sabotage my life for the sake of good material. Hurt someone, break someone's heart and then call it *my story*. For a while, I didn't want to be happy, just in control of my sabotage. This mentality made it easier for me to fall into the typical male traps of lust, chronic dishonesty, and peer pressure. I hurt a lot of people and began to hate who I was becoming. I could barely keep up with the lies I was telling and the person I was pretending to be.

Whether you have relinquished your power to the accuser or accepted that things will simply never change, I want you to ask yourself a question. It's a question my mentor instructs me to ask myself from time to time. *Do I want to be free?* Ask again. Now this one -- *Will I let this keep me from God's plan for me?* Because unhandled pain, un-forgiveness, negativity, distrust, and hatred will keep you from assured joy. Sure, you might get married, have kids, and have a decent career, but will you stop the toxins? In Anneli Rufus's book, *Unworthy*, she talks about how she learned and adopted self-hatred by watching her mother. Everything her mother was afraid of was projected onto her. While this may sound like an extreme example, we can all think of one or two habits that we got from our parents that we may not be proud of. Let's be honest, it's not that crazy of a thought. There is a such thing as generational cycles and generational hurt.

Which brings me back to our point about the bolts that fasten us to the pain -- the rivet. Rivets keep our wounds open. It gives all the clutter we claim we want to get away from the ability to hurt us. It gives the people who we are trying to get rid of access to us. And typically, except in some cases of abuse, we can end it all -- to unfasten the screws and bolts. We just have to follow through. We must stop picking up the phone, stop going to that bar, stop looking at their social media, stop picking fights, stop talking back, stop overthinking. Change the habit. If you typically check this person's social media at night, turn your phone off when you get in bed. If you always get down on yourself when you drink, this is going to sound crazy, but stop drinking! Get an accountability partner, a good friend or family member. Someone who can hold you accountable and not judge you.

My beast was my thought process and my rivet was the poetry. I stopped writing for a period. This allowed me to confront the beast. While I loved writing, it was preventing me from being my best self. I changed my relationship with people around me and started finding ways to love and focus on myself. During this time, I did a lot of self-reflection, reading and praying. God revealed fountains of truth to me during this season. When I felt ready, I picked up the pen with a new sense of purpose and strength. I could extend grace to others who were in the midst of their respective growing processes without judgment. Best of all, I could share my story with others.

Day by day, hour by hour, chance by chance, start to loosen the screws. Start small and make goals. Pray in the mornings, the evenings and any time you feel tempted to tighten the bolts again. Find a scripture to stand on. Elevation requires separation. You need this! When you pray, listen. Stop asking for things and just listen. Allow God to reveal His truth to you. Allow the questions above to fuel you when you're weak or when you feel like you're becoming complacent again. Do not allow the pollution in your heart, all the mistakes you have made, and all the people who have hurt you from being your best self. You deserve what God has for you. Trust me, He wants to give it to you, too.

Make a decision and don't talk yourself out of it. I promise that if you do not decide today, you will keep putting it off. Do not be the person who realizes everything two years later. Leave it. No, seriously, leave it. It's time to exit the lair, their lair, your lair. There's nothing left for you here. Now it's time to conquer the beast.

Confess It

"I've never heard of a man or woman breaking a
debilitating habit without public confession.
Ask the folks at Alcoholics Anonymous.
They'll tell you that going public with a habit is the first
possibly the most important step in recovery. "
Andy Stanley

Serenity

Lord,
Give me
The strength to make peace with my past,
The courage to create a new future,
And the patience required to adorn it with love.

How Excellent

A God who called us beautiful in our ugly phase
    but ain't we all still a little ugly?
And I know that breathing is hard sometimes,
    but ain't He like the escape in an exhale?

A God, who never needed a woman to close her eyes
    for Him to be the man of her dreams,
    who declared you good
    before the world shaped a graven
    image of your likeness.

A God, a carpenter by trade,
    sent to remind us that our heart is
    our greatest toolbox.
And, if we sharpen our ends,
    we can build anything we put our hands to.

A God who never gets tired of giving us chances
    and don't we all just need another one?

A God who painted pieces in the heavens for us
    so that our ancestors would never second-guess
    the direction of their freedom,
    whose hands never quake while He unties
    our souls at night,
    never gets tired of dumping us in Jordans
    and calling us clean,
    or complains about adding foundation in our blemishes.

A God who handcrafted angels for us.
Gave them swords for our doors,
   wings for our eyelids,
   who arrived in our Goliath
   and proclaimed Himself, I AM
   and don't we need Him to be our everything?

Anchors

I was once told that
Sometimes, you just know
That it will anchor your fingertips differently than
We just made it work.

I am of the people who believe that God will use
Our *made it work* to point us to
Our *just know.*

Placeholders

For Irisa
In Christ we are repeatedly chosen, never a placeholder.

I stopped filling my cup
    with half-empty people,
    counting all the ways I would never add up.
The fear of darkness will destroy you faster
    than darkness itself.
    That is to say,
        falling in love with someone's potential,
        the idea of their opulence,
        is much like trying to do surgery on a body
    that you're not even sure is alive.

Have you ever warmed a side of the bed that
    didn't care where you had been?
        Didn't wonder, why you slept
            like you were waiting for something.
    After being a placeholder for so long,
        our bodies tend to reject wholeness.

God did not design souls to be second best.
Ain't give our Spirits permission to
    inhale indigo and inklings of shredded guts.
        Fear idles itself in our idols,
        our tunnel vision of breath.

I've killed myself in the arms of someone
        who loved me 10 times just to be a
        coat hanger for someone 20 more.
                Those nights, I had to remind myself to
                leave my Spirit at home, my
                moral's naiveté.
Truth is like wool when you're forcing
        your skin to live a lie.

And when our feet shuffle mildly
                toward the exit door,
                after time has seasoned us past ripeness,
                        the fruits we now bid whole were
                        just cracking themselves open,
                        planting subordinated seeds.

Your veins are not a pillar in someone's caste system.
        Success is not a substitute for love,
                neither are drugs pillows for loneliness.

Trading My Sorrows

It's never what we let go of
  But what we trade for what God has for us.
It's never about steering
  But trusting God enough to let Him take the wheel.
It's never about the loss
  But about the sweat, the fervor, the survival in our
  testimony.

Our Job

Job 1:20

I fell on my face.
Isn't that what sinners do?

Prodigals who are not sure their fathers
see them from afar.

Yet, I spent 4 1/2 years of university
fabling, fibbing, pretending that God was a genie,

a Scantron, I rubbed my hands on hoping
I didn't binge myself out of an answer.

Failed tests, failed parents, failed you,
a balancing act

Putting lips to books, and curious eyes
to caffeinated blood

Remotes to blind girls
and damaged hearts to safe spaces.

And, I spent 4 1/2 years of university
unlearning my conscience

Which would explain why I'm now on
my face, my closet too full of skeletons

To pray, carpet burn, and wet shame.
Shedding my shell, coaxing the ground.

Mama 'nem said that it is our Job to fall on
our faces.

That is when fires start and rams appear.
And the sky speaks in a language that

only ruin can understand.

Broken Mirrors

Don't be afraid to shatter
who you thought you wanted to be.
And to use bloody hands
to pick up the pieces.
This time you will be much more cautious
about the reflection you create.

An un-watered Love

I remember that winter like it was yesterday.
It was a winter that carried a wind
I didn't even have a jacket for.

A winter that was bleak, bitter and grim.
And the days after, ushered in nightmares
And I never firmly believed that demons could drive
fears, but, sure enough,
I became afraid that damaged relationships not cultivated
in their season would simply die there.
On a warm day the following spring,
desolate thoughts compelled me to revisit my garden
again.

And as I walked, I couldn't help but notice that tracks
once trailed now seemed to be forgotten,
filled with dark grasses whose spirits blamed me
for the fact that they had now been spoiled rotten.
And they were right.
To be completely honest,
I had become so used to people walking out of my life,
that I convinced myself that even the most loyal people
weren't worth the fight.

As I stepped over fences I had so diligently built by hand,
I remember protecting these
bonds like I would never see them again.

I can't say that I was shocked at what I stumbled upon
Withered roots and spoiled fruits found comfort
while I was gone.
Somehow, I had bypassed water pails and even on the
sunniest days I had failed to nurture the relationships
I had been given.
I could never walk in love because
the love inside of me had utterly gone missing.

Stained gloves and empty bottles of pesticides
had specialized as the perfect stand-ins,
remnants of patience for something
I claimed I loved but still found a way to abandon.
She said, *You always give up so easily.*
She was right.

I had become complacent in growing,
fed up with sowing,
tired of digging perfect trenches so I resorted to hoeing.
Quite frankly,
farming wasn't easy and growth wasn't really lucid
and I knew that rain would eventually come
so, I used inclement weather as my excuses.
Immaturity made me walk away when everything was
good, ignoring messages like
Do you love me?
Are you going to call me like you said you would?

Rain checking our progression
until I was left with nothing more
than an empty sound,
a cloud who knew me by name,

drowning inklings of my happiness so that I could soak in
the pain and a darkness that felt sorry for me.
He said,
Even demons know what light looks like, even if it blinds them.
Because an un-watered love is like experiencing every
single season, only for the spring time to never come.
For the sun, to never think you were worth shining for.
An un-watered love is
the question mark that lingers after you ask God why.

But on that day, I found You.
Posted in the middle of my garden.
Bent like You were waiting for me to return.
As I dug away with anger and toiled,
disappointed in all the relationships
I found a way to soil, You comforted me.
Pests could never attest to what kept You grounded.
Even I had infected myself with foolishness that
had intricate ways of keeping me bounded.
Your stem was as strong as barbells and
Your heart was as big as rainbows and as the saying goes,
Don't bury your pain next to what you love because that's
how the pain grows.
You have to find a way to pull it out.
Your roots taught me how to rest steadily in patience.
Even in the darkest hours You created me to grow through
respiration.

I used to be ashamed when bitter fruits
would expose my bad decisions, but
You taught me how to cut them down and
lift them up in forgiveness.
How to sow better, fertilize in faith,

and look at the blessings through the rain
because a good farmer only learns how to plant better,
he doesn't have to throw dirt on anybody's name.

And nowadays I'm happy to be amongst
the same people that I started with.
It's true that the grass is the greenest where you water it.
Learn to love yours and when harvest time comes,
you can eat first and,
before you plant anything close to you,
don't forget to do your research.

I'm no longer inclined to walk away when things
we go through are tough but now
I'm addicted to watering with as much love as I can.
So, I apologize for abandoning you for the smallest
reasons, or looking for better fruits because that's what
seemed to be in season.
In due time, everything that needs to
will find a way to be exposed and
I know that you will, *Never Stop Improving*
so I'm learning to love you at your Lowe's.

God has given us plenty of loving water.
Will you decide to use it? or
Will you walk away when it's the easiest to throw the
deuces? What's mine is ours,
and I thank Him every day for using me
to help you develop your flowers.
So, if you love someone or something,
you can either water it and watch it grow or
abandon the garden of love
long enough for you to see it go.

Sunflower

From you, I have learned
that if we keep our eyes on God
He will be sure to give us all the
things that we prayed about.

I Find It Funny

I had to stop pretending I didn't feel betrayed.
I've tried to forget those days, dark nights
When I could've had you, I declined.
I surprised myself.
Funny how that works.
Sometimes when you have it,
You don't even want it anymore.

Forgiving: A Process

"If God forgives and you don't, that makes you half the man but all the sin"
Jasmine Mans

Trying to extract salt from water before it dissolves
Inhaling for the sake of anger
Exhaling for the possibility of answers
Emptying a ship of bitterness so your heart won't sink
Walking lighter
Attending family dinners with folks you don't consider
family
Cleaning shame from the smudges on your mirror
Sighing deeply to the cadence of falling tears
Shushing your pride
Declining the optimal time to bring up the past
Picking up the phone before the last ring
Unblocking them and blocking them again
Avoiding the argument
Refraining from punishment
Clapping for someone who hurt you
Giving someone the chance to love your scars
Absolving the urge to break their arm while they do it
Loving yourself in places you once hid
Silencing the accuser
Canceling a debt that will never be paid
Praying without a guilty conscious

Sleeping better at night
Remembering that He forgave us first
Forgetting

Yes, forgetting

The word, forgetting, is not condoning a state of denial or naiveté. It is not to say that we should pretend like the past did not happen. But rather, it is to say, that we should not let the memory of the offenses fuel the same hurt that it once caused.

Soda Pop

Lust is the man who
quenches his thirst with soda
because he's never had water before.

Love is the woman who
offers water at no charge
when there are thousands who honor its scarcity.

But some men would rather have soda.
It tastes better with their spirits.

Pimp Lucifer

What is pride?
Pride is the pimp I never became
Coroners who open caskets
for dead praise

Bodies levitating in a
Sea of open wounds
An empty exchange of self
Hovering over a bottomless grave

Hymns beg pardons
Steal harmonies when hubris
is the pallbearer of a damned spirit
Lucifer must be a sculptor

An artist of some sort
Pimp of souls
Because pride
Pride will pimp you

Paint your pedestal
Pirate the producer
Prepare you for the plunge
It is tree, metal, oil, thick grit

State of crowd
With no elbow room
Bench of judge
Gaveling a pit of no reward

No wonder arrogance will
Bury a man before his time
And humility sheds blood
Like eternity is our birthright

Confessions

The poem that cured my Stomach Aches

First off, I'm a sinner.
And I had relationships with demons in their homes
with no intentions of leaving them alone
Because I fell in love with another identity.

And as a young dude,
none of the girls seemed to be into me.
I thought that I wasn't good enough
or hood enough or that
the fact that I didn't have sex stories
made it seem like my game wasn't real enough.
Following the footsteps of my father
didn't seem to bother women
who had never had relationships with their own
So, I went unnoticed and I gave up being a nice guy
because that role was completely hopeless.

Being that virgin in high school
was a reality that I never wanted to believe
so, I lied on sexual encounters just hoping I would be free,
because in locker rooms,
it seemed like being the virgin
was worse than having a STD.

Then came influence, and I saw how easy it does it.
I was the shortest dude so I had no reason to live above it
and when they poured it all up
I didn't realize what had gotten into me.

That's why I ate my pride for breakfast
and got rid of my identity.
I smoked to escape depression but the highs made me
lower and liquor put me in control of women
who I thought I'd never get until I got older.

So over and over, I fell into this repetition of
awakening the hearts of women
and then facing eviction on the search for more attention.
And I became so used to losing and hurting that
I often sabotaged my wins
because I didn't think that I deserved it.
They said,
It only hurts because your appeal is so real
and I thought you would be the man who would
really seal the deal.

But, instead, I punished people for loving me.
Thinking, if they really knew what was out there,
how could they see themselves ending up with me?
I didn't love myself so I lied for acceptance.
I was afraid I wasn't worth the sacrifice
and no one would give me reverence.
I was so afraid of being alone that I knocked
on the walls of women hoping
to make their heart my home,
and I would wine and dine their souls
with images of me being bae but I treated them like hotels.
They were only a temporary stay.

I used women, hiding in swollen veins pretending
to be the man they really wanted
until their heart was completely mended.

As long as we could hit the back seat,
being walked over was fine
and you didn't have to ask me to put myself into recline.
I retreated to corners in battle, running, ducking
fires of my actions,
hoping to find pieces of the fences I had straddled.
And I yearned to hear the words,
I really want to be with you
But if they said *he really ain't it girl,*
then I would probably agree with you.

I was a prisoner to lust
finding satisfaction in sexual agreements
because I was incapable of trust.
And until about now, these things ain't even matter,
I was once your *Sweetest Thing* but
Miseducation turned me into your *Ex-Factor.*

So, I met God at the corner of depression and confession
and asked Him to point me to the right highway
so I could go back to being a blessing.
Tired of hitting road blocks, traveling
where the blood flowed
and He pointed me to Calvary,
redemption soaked my entire soul.
And I shed my old skin on
the rocks of love, faith, and truth
and prayed that if I gave Him my all,
I would come back to you all with proof.

I am a living testimony and
a loser without Christ.
I tried to trade Him out of this game of life

But nothing would ever suffice.

He separated me
from the things that kept us away for so long.
And I'm so proud to say that
I've made His heart my home.

I'm no longer in bondage.
And it no longer confines me.
And now I show the love that He's given
knowing that it will come back and find me.

Realizing now that,
I was always a winner.
Life doesn't just teach us how to find ourselves,
it teaches us how to remember.

So, let us change for love,
let us change for life.
I've had enough of just living life,
now it's time for me to start living right.

I am a man of God.
Living life through His example
and always praying for guidance
for things that I can't handle.

I put it all away so that
He would stir, shake, and rearrange me.
I'm so sorry that you could never enjoy,
the completely changed me.

Interlude 4

A Session for Confessions

There is no freedom where there is no confession.

We are almost there. Now it is time to confront the beast. You may have noticed in the other piece, I said that once I identified my toxic relationship with my craft, I was able to tell others about it. You may have heard from a wise parent or perhaps an overzealous Sunday school teacher that the *truth will set you free*. Cliché of course, but this fact is undeniable. While the truth may cost us short term gratification, it will not cost us our freedom. Everyone who is a slave is a slave to a lie -- a lie about life, about themselves, about God or their behavior. I do not have to remind you (but I will) that any lie we tell will only force us into more bondage. This is not only physical bondage, but also mental and emotional bondage. Telling, living, or believing lies about yourself is the quickest way to end up six feet deep.

Let us revisit the question. How do we conquer the beast? We confess. When we confess, the beast can no longer keep us in the lair. When we confess, the accuser can no longer torture us about the things that we have already accepted and plan to change about ourselves and our current situation. Confession is scary because, when we confess, we are now responsible for the truth that comes to light. We can no longer hide behind the excuse,

I didn't know. While my confession came during restoration, yours might come before. Do what your heart is telling you to do here. Be vulnerable. Say it aloud. Listen to yourself and God. Weed out the cushion that makes it sound nice. Confess it to God, yourself, your loved ones, your significant other, and, most importantly, make a plan to fix it. You will fail numerous times and that's okay. Keep at it. Write a note to yourself, pray about it, and when the time arises, ignore the stomach aches and do what you said you were going to do. Beware. The beast will try to make you feel guilty, like a traitor, or even unworthy of your new life. The comfort zone you have built in the lair must be left behind as well. Most times, lies attach themselves to things that we cherish, and the beast will dangle that in front of us. But do not be deceived, your true happiness is not in this place.

If you fail, do not beat yourself up. My good friend, Rob, always reminds me that we should never punish ourselves for something more than once, even when others try to do it again and again. And trust me, they will try. When the accuser returns, do not be afraid to tell him verbally (yes, aloud) that he has no power in your life and in your mind. Do this every single time it happens, until your thoughts start lining up with what you are saying. Your words will be your strongest weapon here.

Most of all, fill your ears and heart with good things. Read and listen to what God says about you in His Word. Keep good company, positive friends, coworkers, and family. You will need people who will side with the new you, the you that is changing.

Careful

I am becoming conscious of the love that I seek.

Careful not to look for things that will knock me off,
But, instead, put me back on my feet.

Something New

Your lips are as soft as peace and
Your smile reminds me of Christmas morning.

And if someone told me months ago
that I would share this moment with someone like you
I can't say that I would've believed them,
but I do think that I would've slept better at night.
Because cold words have a way of sticking to your bones,
no matter how warm your sheets are.
A guilty conscience is like feeding a monster
that will never get full,
And a restless heart,
A restless heart is the nightmare that plays while your
eyes are wide open.

And I'll admit it,
I'm guilty of looking for the right things
in all the wrong places.
I'll admit that doubting love could love me too
is what made me okay with being complacent.

But you, you are my what if.
You are the manifestation of my imagination,
The answer to a prayer that I was too embarrassed
to bring up again.

Simply Because

I have reserved pieces of my heart for you.
Locked them up and stored them in my lungs
Simply because,
I am not afraid to breathe you.

Yellow Signs

"I fell in love the way you fall asleep: slowly, and then all at once"
John Green

We ate at Waffle House
like it was our first time eating breakfast
after a night of spontaneous romance.
And while that wasn't the case,
I knew that this would be the night I would say
I love you.
But I didn't know how.
Gritty teeth, stomach burdened
Cheeks too tired from smiles
Head too stubborn to believe
Breaths too short to catch
Eyes too flustered to focus
Hands aching for something longer than a thought
to hold on to.

When we parted, your smile shined like the last
good thing God would ever give me
before my kids.
I learned that it's never just about the length of
the hug but the rock in the embrace.
But the words would never free fall from
my lips that night.
The moment felt too much like a dream
and I wanted to pace myself.
Like eating a sweet treat slowly as a child,
we leaned on each other like poles on playgrounds
trying to figure out who would let go first.

The *I love you too* you sent back in the text
made me feel like a fool.
Foolish enough to have let that moment slip away.
Foolish enough to believe that there is God
who knew that I needed you.

Geneva

To the grandfather that I never had the pleasure of understanding

I think that you might be proud of me now.
My only regret is that I never really knew you
Why rum and coke was your favorite dessert,
why money was the only thing you seemed to be afraid
to lose.

Were you ever afraid that you would lose us?
That we would lose faith in your words,
satisfaction in your advice?
That our hearts would never recognize that we meant
something to you.

Your watch is a reminder,
That while time may be with us,
it may very well be against us.
The certainty that it will move forward,
but the uncertainty in what it will bring.

I finally put a battery in it last week.
So that maybe after ten years,
I would finally feel worthy enough of your time.

Man Down

I was always under the assumption that manning up was tying your own shoes, stopping all that crying all the time, pretending to like a girl, liking a girl and then pretending not to like her anymore. Fighting, being good at sports, paying for things, being good with your hands, putting a condom on gracefully, pretending like you already had sex even though you're a virgin. A whole lot of pretending, pretending not to feel, not to be jealous, to be satisfied, to be secure, to be unafraid. This is perhaps the one I hated the most -- pretending that men should never be afraid of anything, which is absurd. When we pretend, we live in a state of subconscious fear and when we fear, we rarely acknowledge and when we don't acknowledge, when we are inevitably damaged by life's upsets, we don't heal. And I'm not even sure that manning up includes the process of healing. Instead, it is working through pain, splitting wounds back open and bragging about it to anyone who will listen. It is the inflammation of pride that denies help and rejects vulnerability.

The damage of this rhetoric is running amuck in the voices of our boys. The walls and defense mechanisms they will build because we will not allow them to feel will only make it harder for the people who attempt to love them later in their lives. By forcing them to pledge themselves to an empty standard of experience, we deny them the ability to love themselves. Instead, they begin to protect the man we have forced them to revere and regard, the ego. All of this shaping, only to find out when he is older, that the personification of this ego, will only stunt his intimacy with his God, his mate and his family.

I've done quite a bit of manning and very few of the experiences I mentioned above will shape true character. If telling someone to man up is to say protect me, love me, defend me, or honor me, then perhaps we should just say that. There is a lot of false rhetoric circulating about the behavior that this term should render. Perhaps, we should understand what a loving, Godly man should be before we utter this phrase again.

iDance

God gave me a reason   to find comfort in my
seasons

To purify my heart   get rid of demons.

          Give me Your heart.

Strengthen   my soul to replenish.

Use me with Your love   so that I can make a
difference.

Thank You for patience.

          I have lit candles in my heart for
You.

Thank You for strength.

          I dance in heart, smile in soul.

Thank You for grace.

          I sleep better at night now.

Thank You for love.

          I am no longer afraid
to come up short.

A Letter to My First Love

"Life isn't a support system for art. It's the other way around"
Stephen King

All the lost boys in me are ready to return home
    Dawn arises around this suit like the
        night's best kept secret
            This will all be over soon

Every orphan locked inside the prison of my bones
    has conspired against his sentence
    An appeal has never tasted so uniform

I have experienced demons
    that will play puppet with your fingertips
        Put you in a cage with your handwritten waiver
          Don't Screwtape your tongue
            Your godliness is half spit, half swallow

I found my calling
    Like Paul and Silas, praised my prison into debris
        Set my captives free
            Turned my morning into dancing
               Embarked upon Damascus in my first
               poem
                  the King transfigured my handprint

The warden on the other side of this stylus
　　penned a letter
　　　　mailed his prisoners and it went:

I cannot recall who put us here.
But,

I will no longer sabotage for your namesake,
Destroy in your honor.
I will no longer walk around covered in Band-Aids.
I deserve to be healed.

I can no longer lay on the altar for you,
Burn myself for display,
Disappear in the smoke...

I deserve to live.

My eyes casted their burdens
　　as I watched glory dissipate from the page
　　　　Our destiny is always waiting for us
　　　　　　even after we've written ourselves off

Your calling beckons you now
　　It will knock the balls of your heels
　　　　until you transform your walk

This Joy

When you get dressed in the morning,
Do you pick your clothes based on
how you look on the outside
Or how you feel on the inside?
Or maybe you just put on whatever's clean.

Have you ever put a costume of happiness
on a body of shame?
Placed a hat on a head of sorrow?
Have you ever put makeup on a face
that wasn't quite dry from the night before?

Or have you ever put on a watch
that gave you time and you couldn't lose it?
Fastened up belt that still hasn't allowed you to prove it?
Have you ever tied up sneakers
that still haven't encouraged you to Just Do It?

Sometimes our happy endings come
before we've stepped out the house that day.
Labeled by these dirty rags, fake tags,
and lately I've been searching for a joy I've never had...
And on those mornings, after we've tried to
dress it up and make it real for our futures,
If we listen, the faintest whisper of hope,

will ask us this great question.
Son, baby girl, who even told you that you were naked?

I wish that laughter came as often as pain
or that sunshine affected my mood
just as much as the rain.
I have a question for the heavens.
Does the Sun ever get upset at how
uneasy the clouds make us about our plans or
ambivalent of how much more slippery it makes our
hands?

Does it ever anger him at how,
on rainy days, the world slows down even
just for a moment...
To ponder on if everything on our agenda
that day is even worth the hassle?
Or would we much rather be doing something
more meaningful, more peaceful?...

I have faith in Him.
I would bet that the Sun doesn't get jealous
But, instead, finds peace in the fact that
God allows him to kiss us.
To lift us.
To put us in his gravity and never attempt to dismiss us.
I wish that we could be as grateful as the Sun.

I remember when happiness would await me
at the entrance of restaurants,
Wishing I had more bubble gum than
my mouth could chew,
Enough friends to take over the world because
how can we pretend to be X-Men with just us two?
Dreams of pushing our wheels like Pinky and the Brain.
I remember wishing that I had just 5 more minutes
at Ben Hill.
It seemed like I had so much more to do.
Or wishing I could run faster from bullies
even when respect seemed to be the only thing
I had to lose.
I wish that happiness was enough.

But like those clothes, you tend to outgrow it.
Like a couple more pounds,
it will begin to weigh you down and at first,
you will be the only one to notice.
So, you spend countless hours in the mirror
trying to get your soul to remember
what you look like naked but its memory has left you,
left with your peace and now all you have left is pieces.
Now you're looking for a size that's bigger,
that, that temporal fixer.
Finding so much comfort in the loudness of our desires,
that we lose the truth in its whisper.

Because living with happiness and no joy is like
carrying the finest wallet but having no money to put in it.
Going broke over an emotion that was never meant
to keep you full.
So, you go to sleep on an empty stomach.
And Lord knows that I have fallen asleep
with a smile on my face and waken up with tears.
Lord knows that I tried to play the game of life
without my joystick, I've done it for years.

Lord knows that sometimes a smile is
just a crying face that wasn't brave enough
to make an appearance
until someone asks if you're okay...
You felt like you had to hide it
because your outfit was too nice that day.
Too afraid that if you had to wear your pain
like your skin tone,
they would look at you that way.
Thank goodness that you practiced.

But joy,
When I was a child,
they would tell me to jump for you,
but they never explained how to do it
when my feet got weary.

Joy,

Are you still where Lauryn left you?

If Zion was a mile away,

I would pack up my bags and leave this world behind.

Joy,

Sometimes,

I can feel you bud out of the shame of my skin.

You are the fruit of my spirit that

no woman has ever tasted.

So, I want to take this time out to thank God

for giving me something that

the world did not give to me,

And something that they can never take away.

Thank you, God, for warming up my heart

when I was too cold to take a deep breath.

Thank you, God, for dialing up joy,

and putting it in my bed when I thought that

sorrow was the only thing that knew my sleep number.

Thank you, God, for taking my emotions to the park

Because sometimes they just needed some fresh air

and a new outlook.

Joy,

You have delivered me from the

things we buy to cover up what's inside.

Joy,
I have waited on you like John did Jesus.
Because men will need you when
they become brave enough to walk on water.

Joy,
I will find comfort in you like
broken hearts on sunken pillows.
Because I know that you will be there
to wake me up in the morning.

Joy,
I love the way you dance in the echoes of my praise.

And I wish,
No, I thank you for remaining the same way

From the rising of the sun to the going down of the same.

You do not need it. It does not serve you.

You are free.

Thank you, God, for ridding us of all
the things that will keep us from our purpose.

About the Author

John Wood is a writer and poet from Southwest Atlanta. Upon graduating the University of Georgia, he launched his poetry brand SpokenWood, a narrative dedicated to unveiling the stories of the young black male. Wood's poems are centered around the subjects of love, spirituality, growth, and identity and his dialogue is unique. His words provide a platform of honesty, self-reflection, and healing to any soul that is in search of truth. Wood thrives in the Atlanta area, performing at events and open mics across the city. He has performed alongside names like GeorgiaMe (Def Poetry Jam) and Alysia Harris (Striver's Row).